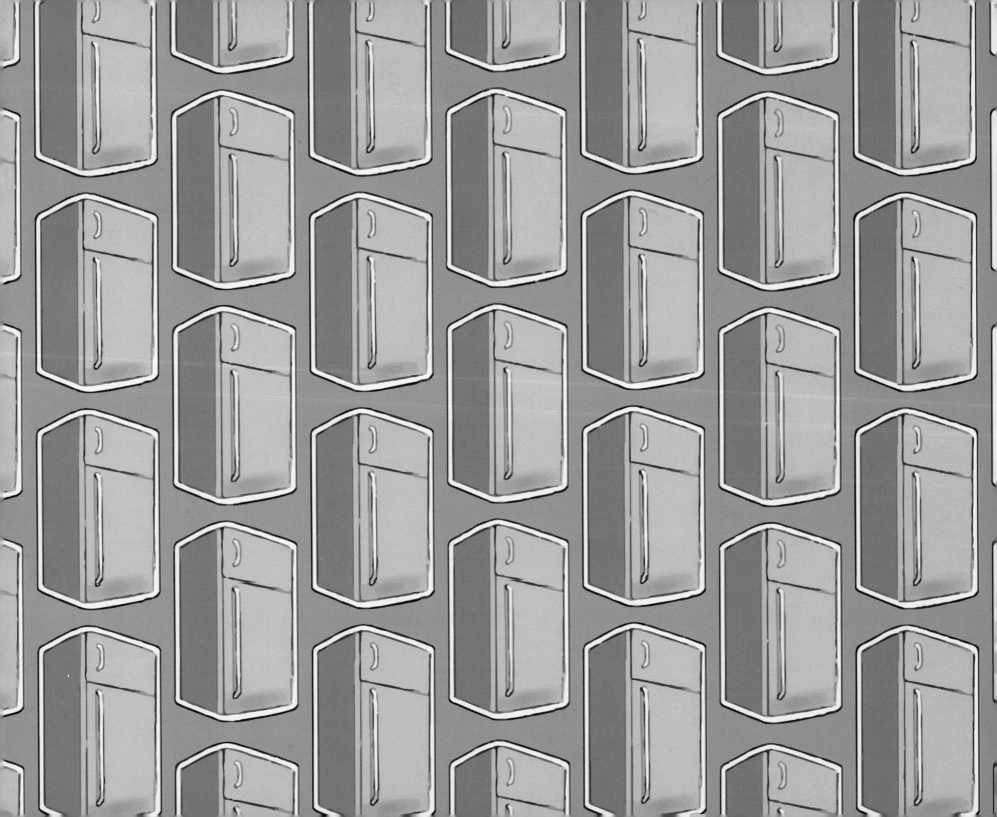

PAGE PUBLISHING, INC.
New York, NY

First originally published by Page Publishing, Inc. 2019

ISBN 978-1-64584-368-9 (Paperback)
ISBN 978-1-64584-370-2 (Hardcover)
ISBN 978-1-64584-369-6 (Digital)

Printed in the United States of America

THIS BOOK BELONGS TO:

SCRAPS' FOOD GUIDE

FROM A ➡ Z

Damon Versaggi

It's never too early or too late
to start developing a healthy
relationship with food.

— V

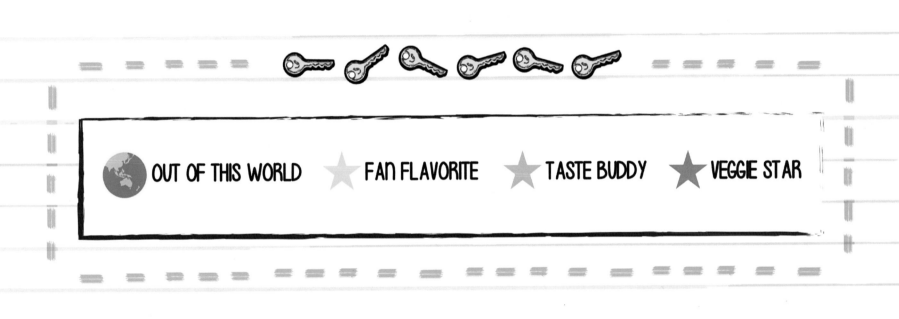

OUT OF THIS WORLD ⭐ FAN FLAVORITE ⭐ TASTE BUDDY ⭐ VEGGIE STAR

A:

– IS FOR –

AVOCADO

★ ★ ★

SCRAPPYFACTS

Sprinkle some lemon juice on avocados to keep them fresh.

1

B: —IS FOR— BEETROOT

SCRAPPYFACTS

Beet juice can be used as a natural fabric dye.

C

— IS FOR —

CARROT

SCRAPPYFACTS

Carrots can help improve eyesight and skin health.

D:

— IS FOR —

DUMPLINGS

SCRAPPYFACTS

Leftovers make great fillings for homemade dumpling.

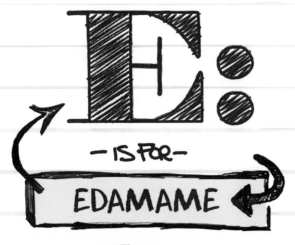

— IS FOR —

EDAMAME

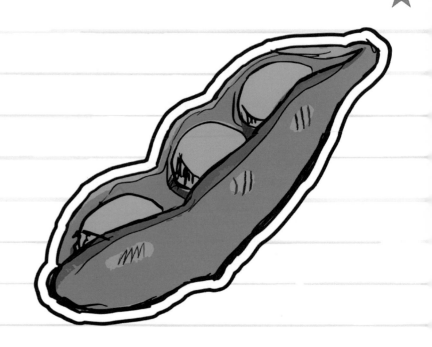

SCRAPPYFACTS

Edamame means "beans on a branch" in Japanese.

F: -IS FOR- FREEZE YOUR FOOD

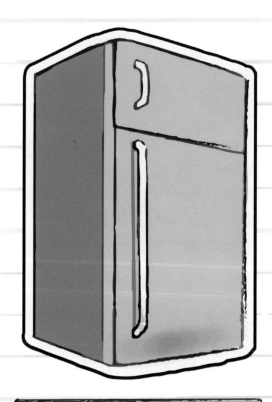

SCRAPPYFACTS

Freezing your food is a great way to get more life out of your meals.

G

— IS FOR —

GAZPACHO

SCRAPPYFACTS

Gazpacho is a term for a cold soup with a vegetable or fruit base.

H:

— IS FOR —

HUMMUS

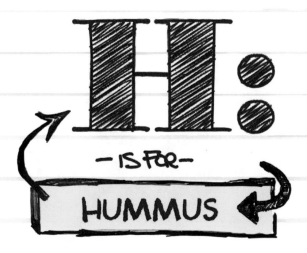

SCRAPPYFACTS

Hummus is made from chickpeas, which are high in plant-based protein.

I:
— IS FOR —
ICEBERG LETTUCE

SCRAPPYFACTS

Iceberg lettuce makes for a healthy burger bun substitute.

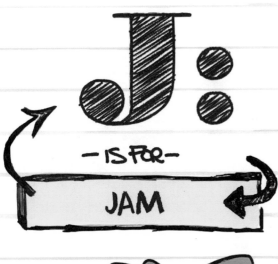

J:

- IS FOR -

JAM

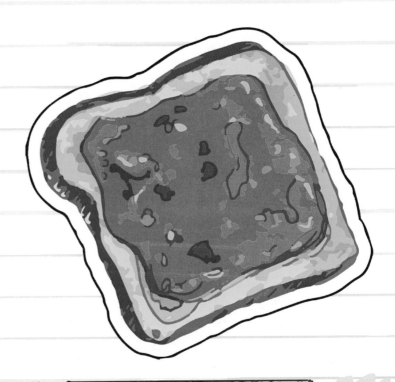

SCRAPPYFACTS

A typical jar of jam should last up to a year after it's opened.

K: — IS FOR — KIWI

SCRAPPYFACTS

A quick and easy way to peel a kiwifruit is with a teaspoon.

L: — IS FOR — LASAGNA

SCRAPPYFACTS

The first lasagna recipe can be traced back to the 14th century.

M: —IS FOR— MANGO

SCRAPPYFACTS

More fresh mangoes are eaten around the world every day than any other fruit.

N:
— IS FOR —
NORI

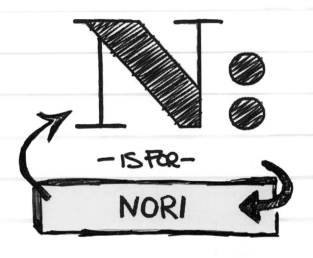

SCRAPPYFACTS

Nori, a type of seaweed, is one of the world's most nutritious crops.

— IS FOR —

ORANGE SALAD

SCRAPPYFACTS

"Insalata di arance" is a Sicilian dish that combines oranges with olive oil, salt and pepper.

P:

— IS FOR —
PIZZA

SCRAPPYFACTS

You can make a pizza crust out of vegetables, like cauliflower and potato.

Q:
— IS FOR —
QUAIL EGG

SCRAPPYFACTS

Smaller quail eggs have more nutritional value than chicken eggs.

R:

— IS FOR —

RAMEN

SCRAPPYFACTS

Slurping noodles, such as ramen, is considered polite and is a compliment to the chef.

- IS FOR -

SQUASH

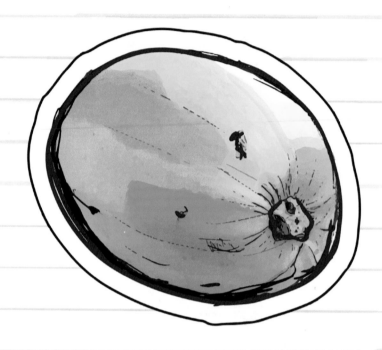

SCRAPPYFACTS

Spaghetti squash can be used as a pasta substitute.

T: —IS FOR— TACOS

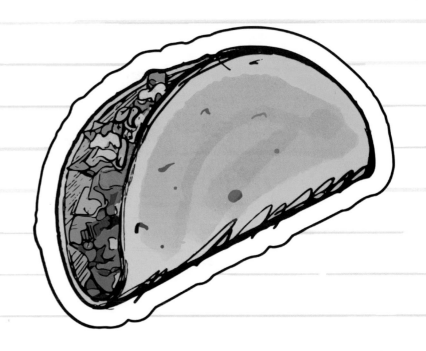

SCRAPPYFACTS

Try enhancing tacos by adding something pickled like onions or jalapeños.

U: —IS FOR— UMAMI

SCRAPPYFACTS

Umami is a savory taste, that's also one of the five basic flavors.

V:

—IS FOR—

VANILLA

SCRAPPYFACTS

Vanilla is one of the most expensive spices in the world.

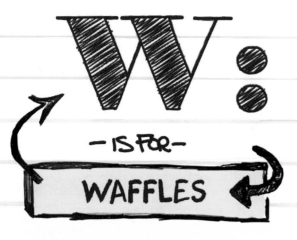

W:
– IS FOR –
WAFFLES

SCRAPPYFACTS

Oat milk is a dairy-free milk alternative that is great for making waffles fluffy.

23

X:

— IS FOR —

X-TRA SPICY

SCRAPPYFACTS

Hot peppers, like habaneros, are great foods for jump starting your metabolism.

Y **:**

—IS FOR—

YAMS

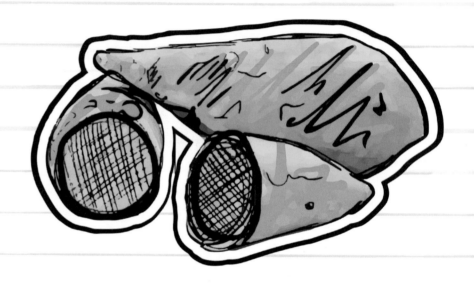

SCRAPPYFACTS

Unlike most vegetables, yams are available all year long.

Z: — IS FOR —

ZUCCHINI BLOSSOMS

SCRAPPYFACTS

These edible flowers are great lightly battered and pan fried.

About the Author

Damon Versaggi is a Brooklyn born and bred artist who has always loved and appreciated the opportunities that food has to offer. While in art school, he worked at restaurants and catering halls but decided to pursue a career in 3-D to satisfy his creative appetite. While working in television, Damon realized his passion and decided to start Scrappy Meals in January 2016.

Scrappy Meals is a food agency that aims to change the way people look at and think about food through various creative events, classes, dinners, and more.

This book is dedicated to all the people that Damon has stumbled upon throughout his life in food, television, and everywhere in between. He would like to thank all those people for their continued support and hopes that you all enjoy this book and are happy in your kitchen!

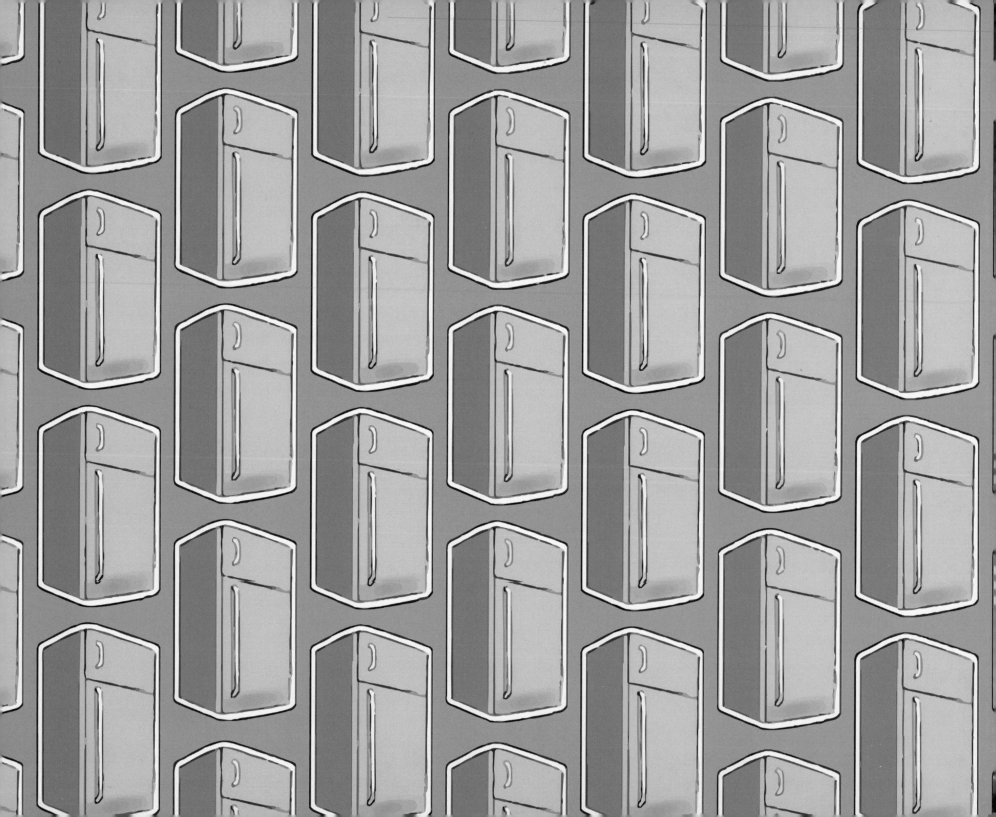